Personal Trainer Practice Test

4th Edition

Joe Cannon, MS

Joe-Cannon.com

Supplement-Geek.com

Copyright and Legal Stuff

Copyright 2015 by Joe Cannon of <u>Joe-Cannon.com</u>.

Disclaimer

Table of Contents

What Others Are Saying About This Test

Holly Chisholm Hargrave, BA, MBA

Founder and CEO www.AthleticGenius.com

Joe Cannon's *Personal Trainer Practice Test* guide is the BEST tool I have ever utilized to prepare myself for a fitness exam. I am a Master Personal Trainer with sixteen international certifications, so trust me—I have taken many a practice test that ill-prepared me . . . Joe cuts to the chase . . . With clarity he communicates exactly what you need to know to perform well on your exam. I wouldn't consider another source other than Joe Cannon.

Wajeeha El Bey, CPT, CHHC, AADP

www.TheSoulisticCircle.com

I initially failed my ACE exam by seven points! Joe reached out via Facebook to me and gave me his test. The test really pulled out the main concepts I needed. The questions were well-written and narrowed down my focus. These are some of the best example test questions you will find passed my ACE exam twelve days later and know it was with Joe's support. Get this test. You won't regret it.

Greg Sims, Co-founder of the Interactive Fitness Trainers Association

www.ifta-fitness.com

Joe Cannon's Personal Trainer Practice Test is well designed and thorough in content. From beginning to end I found it to be functional, just like his text "Personal Fitness Training: Beyond the Basics." I especially liked the way it was broken down into sections and the scoring system that allows you to really understand what you need to study in order to improve. I would recommend it to anyone who is studying for a Personal Trainer test — or anyone who wants to improve their test taking ability.

William Sukala, PhD

www.DrBillSukala.com.au

As both a clinical exercise physiologist and former presenter of the American Council on Exercise exam preparation course, I can guarantee that Joe Cannon's practice test is an excellent resource to facilitate the studying process. If you understand the science behind WHY the correct answers are correct, you will have a decided edge when you sit your exam.

Joanne Smith-Tavener, M.Ed., CSCS*D

Wellness Coordinator, NJSP and AAAI/ISMA Faculty Instructor

www.BreastCancerAndExercise.com

I have been in the fitness industry for over twenty years, and as a fellow AAAI/ISMA faculty instructor, I would highly recommend the use of this practice exam in preparing for our Personal Fitness Instructor Exam. It is comprehensive in its content and focuses on the primary topics of study.

Dwayne Wimmer

Owner, Vertex Fitness Personal Training Studio

www.VertexFit.com

Great job, Joe, putting together one of the most comprehensive practice tests I have seen in the fitness industry. If someone knew the information in the five sections— Exercise Science, Anatomy & Physiology, Fitness Testing, Exercise Program Design, and Nutrition & Sports Nutrition—I feel they would be well on their way to understanding what they need to know to be a professional in the fitness industry. I highly recommend using this Personal Trainer Practice Test as a resource for anyone starting into the fitness industry as a personal trainer.

Jessica Lewis, CPFT, CNC

www.SculptUrLife.com

Joe has such an outstanding track record for training the trainers, it's no surprise that his Practice Test crosses all major fitness organizations' curriculums and is LOADED with real-life information.

Mike Rickett M.S., C.S.C.S., C.S.P.S.

www.MichaelRickett.com

This test provides an efficient way to prepare for fitness certifications through any organization. It's also a great way to review your knowledge and practice your test-taking abilities.

Debra Mazda, ME.d., CPT

President/CEO, ShapelyGirl Fitness

www.ShapelyGirlFitness.com

Without hesitation, I can say that Joe's knowledge of fitness, exercise, and science is outstanding. Joe is my go-to guy when I have any questions about nutrition, research, health, or fitness. I highly recommend anything that he writes.

About The Author

I'm Joe Cannon, and I created this practice test to help give you an idea of some of the information you will need to be familiar with as a personal trainer and, hopefully, to help you pass a fitness certification exam.

I have an MS degree in exercise science and a BS degree in chemistry and biology. As for certifications, I am a CSCS and NSCA-CPT. I've worked in health clubs and I have been self-employed since about 2002.

Today, I am a personal trainer, teacher, blogger, and consultant.

What sets me apart from others is that I *train the trainers*. I TEACH personal training and sports nutrition seminars and have done so for over a decade. This gives me a unique insight into what trainers know *and* don't know. In fact, some of the questions I've been asked in class have been used in this test to make it more realistic. This test contains real-life questions that you might not find elsewhere.

Previously, I've written several other books. You can learn more about all of them here:

http://www.joe-cannon.com/books

On my personal website, I write A LOT about personal training. Take advantage of it. I discuss issues that very few others do. My goal is simple: ***I want you to know what I know.*** That way, you can avoid the mistakes others have made—including me.

Ok, enough about me, let's talk about the practice test…

About this Practice Test

This practice test has **300 questions**. It is divided into five sections. These are the main sections covered on most fitness certification tests:

1. Exercise Science: 60 questions
2. Anatomy & Physiology: 60 questions
3. Fitness Testing: 60 questions
4. Exercise Program Design: 60 questions
5. Nutrition & Sports Nutrition: 60 questions

The answers to all the questions are listed at the end of this book.

Scoring the Test

To pass a section, you need a score of **at least 80%.** You can score each section separately at the end of the test. That way, you can see if there are any areas where you need to improve.

How to Take This Test

Take the test in private. Turn off your cell phone and other distractions. Get a calculator too. Use a stopwatch. Remember, most fitness certification tests have a time limit.

Resources Page

I've created a Resources Page for this test. You can see it here:

http://www.joe-cannon.com/test-resources

The Resources Page has additional information to help you achieve your goal of becoming a personal trainer.

Top 25 Tips

This test also includes my Top 25 Tips to help you prepare for the actual certification test you will take. The tips are located at the end of this test.

Any questions? Just email me. I answer all emails personally.

When you're ready, turn the page and let's begin the test.

Exercise Science Section

1. **The aerobic energy system is also called:**

   a.   Glycolysis . . . . ☐

   b.   Krebs cycle . . . . ☐

   c.   ATP/CP . . . . ☐

   d.   Creatine system . . . . ☐

2. **Muscle fibers are grouped into bundles called:**

   a.   Endomysium . . . . ☐

   b.   Fasciculus . . . . ☐

   c.   Myostatic bundle . . . . ☐

   d.   None are correct. . . . . ☐

3. **The contractile unit of a muscle fiber is called:**

   a.   GTO . . . . ☐

   b.   H zone . . . . ☐

   c.   Sarcomere . . . . ☐

   d.   Myofillament . . . . ☐

4. **The cellular reservoir of calcium for muscle cell contraction is found in the:**

   a.   Sarcomere junction . . . . ☐

   b.   Sarcoplasmic reticulum . . . . ☐

   c.   Calcium basin . . . . ☐

   d.   None are correct. . . . . ☐

5. **The breakdown of ATP is:**

   a.   Aerobic . . . . ☐

   b.   Anaerobic . . . . ☐

   c.   Both A and C are correct . . . . ☐

   d.   None are correct. . . . . ☐

6. **Calcium alters the shape of which protein to facilitate muscle contraction?**

   a.   Actin . . . . ☐

   b.   Myostatin . . . . ☐

   c.   Troponin . . . . ☐

   d.   Myosin . . . . ☐

7. **To which protein do cross bridges attach during muscle contraction?**

   a.   Fasciculus . . . . ☐

    b.   The H zone . . . . ☐

    c.   Myofibers . . . . ☐

    d.   None are correct. . . . . ☐

8. The enzyme that breaks down ATP is called:

    a.   ATP enzyme. . . . . ☐

    b.   ATPase . . . . ☐

    c.   No enzyme is needed . . . . ☐

    d.   Myostatin . . . . ☐

9. The muscle fiber that contracts the fastest is:

    a.   Type I . . . . ☐

    b.   Type Ia . . . . ☐

    c.   Type IIb . . . . ☐

    d.   Type IIa . . . . ☐

10. In muscle physiology, the A band is to myosin what the I band is to:

    a.   Sarcomere . . . . ☐

    b.   Actin . . . . ☐

    c.   B band . . . . ☐

    d.   Purkinje . . . . ☐

11. The fiber type that shows the most hypertrophy is:

    a.   Type I . . . . ☐

    b.   Type II . . . . ☐

    c.   Type III . . . . ☐

    d.   Both A and C are correct . . . . ☐

12. Activity not related to formal exercise is called:

    a.   EPOC. . . . . ☐

    b.   NEAT. . . . . ☐

    c.   Isokinetic . . . . ☐

    d.   None are correct. . . . . ☐

13. Fat is broken down for fuel in this area of the cell:

    a.   Sarcoplasmic reticulum . . . . ☐

    b.   Mitochondria . . . . ☐

    c.   Myostatin system . . . . ☐

    d.   Nucleus . . . . ☐

14. The following muscle fiber type that generates the most power is:

    a.   Type I . . . . ☐

    b.   Type Ia . . . . ☐

    c.   Type IIa . . . . ☐

    d.   Type IIb . . . . ☐

15. Which muscle fiber type would be used the most during a marathon (26.2 miles)?

    a.   Slow twitch, type IIa . . . . ☐

    b.   Slow twitch, type I . . . . ☐

    c.   Fast twitch, type I . . . . ☐

    d.   Fast twitch, type IIb . . . . ☐

16. The act of holding the breath while weight lifting is called:

    a.   Maximal inhalation . . . . ☐

    b.   Orthostatic hypotension . . . . ☐

    c.   Valsalva maneuver . . . . ☐

    d.   VO2 max . . . . ☐

17. The theory that best explains how muscles work is called:

    a.   Sarcoplasmic recycling theory . . . . ☐

    b.   Myostatin regeneration theory . . . . ☐

    c.   Sliding filament theory . . . . ☐

    d.   Myosin cross-bridge theory . . . . ☐

18. The loss of muscle strength and size as we get older is called:

    a.   Atrophy . . . . ☐

    b.   Hyperplasia . . . . ☐

    c.   Myopenia . . . . ☐

    d.   Sarcopenia . . . . ☐

19. The best way to avoid the Valsalva maneuver is:

    a.   Contract the abs . . . . ☐

    b.   Strengthen the rotator cuff . . . . ☐

    c.   Breath during exercise . . . . ☐

    d.   None are correct . . . . ☐

20. Hypertrophy refers to an:

    a.   Increase in myostatin content . . . . ☐

    b.   Increase in muscle size. . . . . ☐

    c.   Increase in muscle cell number . . . . ☐

    d.   Increase in Purkinje fiber number . . . . ☐

21. **A term that refers to an increase in cell muscle cell number is:**

    a.   Hypertrophy . . . . ☐

    b.   Myotrophy . . . . ☐

    c.   Hyperplasia . . . . ☐

    d.   Sarcoplasm . . . . ☐

22. **Which might you expect in a person who runs three miles a day, four days a week?**

    a.   High blood pressure at rest . . . . ☐

    b.   Low resting heart rate . . . . ☐

    c.   Decreased VO2 max . . . . ☐

    d.   Both B and C are correct . . . . ☐

23. **A person from Pennsylvania trains in Colorado for three months. What would be expected?**

    a.   Decreased calorie burning. . . . . ☐

    b.   Increased RBC concentration . . . . ☐

    c.   Decreased RBC concentration . . . . ☐

    d.   Both A and B are correct . . . . ☐

24. **In exercise science, DOMS refers to:**

    a.   Female athletic triad. . . . . ☐

    b.   Dehydration . . . . ☐

    c.   Type I fiber dominance . . . . ☐

    d.   Muscle soreness . . . . ☐

25. **A healthy twenty-five-year-old joins a boot camp fitness class. The next day he notices that his urine is dark-brown coloreWhat might you suspect?**

    a.   DOMS . . . . ☐

    b.   Dehydration . . . . ☐

    c.   Rhabdomyolysis. . . . . ☐

    d.   Excess B vitamins in the diet . . . . ☐

26. **In exercise, the acronym EPOC refers to:**

    a.   Increased breathing rate that occurs after exercise . . . . ☐

    b.   The time period after the active rest phase in periodization . . . . ☐

    c.   Decrease in metabolic rate. . . . . ☐

    d.   None are correct. . . . . ☐

27. Metabolic rate can be viewed as being composed of:

    a.   RMR x blood pressure . . . . ☐

    b.   Cardiovascular + strength training. . . . . ☐

    c.   Anabolism + catabolism . . . . ☐

    d.   VO2 max x blood pressure . . . . ☐

28. The amount of blood pumped from the heart per minute is called:

    a.   Ejection fraction . . . . ☐

    b.   Ejection output . . . . ☐

    c.   Cardiac output . . . . ☐

    d.   Stoke volume . . . . ☐

29. A common effect of the Valsalva maneuver is:

    a.   Increased VO2 max . . . . ☐

    b.   Increased BP . . . . ☐

    c.   Increased muscle endurance. . . . . ☐

    d.   Increased capillary oxygen extraction . . . . ☐

30. A general term that refers to the loss of muscle size and strength is:

    a.   Sarcopenia. . . . . ☐

    b.   Myopenia . . . . ☐

    c.   Atrophy . . . . ☐

    d.   Hypotrophy . . . . ☐

31. Which is best for improving a person's ability to perform push-ups?

    a.   Push-ups . . . . ☐

    b.   Bench press, four sets, 80% 1RM . . . . ☐

    c.   Supersets: pushups/pull ups . . . . ☐

    d.   DB bench press, three sets, 75% 10RM . . . . ☐

32. In exercise science, METs stands for:

    a.   Metabolic exercise thermogenesis . . . . ☐

    b.   Metabolic equivalents . . . . ☐

    c.   Measured exercise time . . . . ☐

    d.   My exercise time . . . . □

33. The cells that carry oxygen through the blood are:

    a.   White blood cells . . . . □

    b.   Erythrocytes . . . . □

    c.   Red blood cells . . . . □

    d.   Both B and C are correct . . . . □

34. Which best describes the effect of chronic exercise on blood pressure?

    a.   No change in BP . . . . □

    b.   Lower BP . . . . □

    c.   Increase BP . . . . □

    d.   Cannot be determined without knowing HR max . . . . □

35. Another name for fast oxidative glycolytic (FOG) muscle fibers is:

    a.   Type I . . . . □

    b.   Type IIa . . . . □

    c.   Type IIb . . . . □

    d.   FOG isn't a muscle fiber type . . . . □

36. In general, which is true about selectorized strength training machines?

    a.   Variable resistance . . . . □

    b.   Constant resistance . . . . □

    c.   Same resistance as free weights . . . . □

    d.   Provide isokinetic resistance only . . . . □

37. Which of the following is not a skeletal muscle?

    a.   Latissimus dorsi . . . . □

    b.   Humerus . . . . □

    c.   Gastrocnemius . . . . □

    d.   All are correct . . . . □

38. Which applies to lactic acid?

    a.   Causes DOMS . . . . □

    b.   Waste product . . . . □

    c.   Made by burning carbs aerobically during exercise . . . . □

    d.   None are correct . . . . □

39. The best time to use a weight lifting belt is:

a.   Always during 15 RM lifts . . . . □

b.   When max stress is placed on low back . . . . □

c.   Only during bench press . . . . □

d.   Always during 20 RM lifts . . . . □

40. Which is true concerning children and exercise?

a.   They sweat sooner than adults. □

b.   They sweat less than adults . . . . □

c.   They take longer to sweat than adults . . . . □

d.   Both B and C are correct . . . . □

41. The process by which electrical signals from the CNS are transmitted to the muscles, causing them to contract is called:

a.   Contraction coupling . . . . □

b.   Sliding filament theory . . . . □

c.   Excitation/contraction coupling. . . . . □

d.   None are correct. . . . . □

42. The chemical which transmits impulses from the CNS to the muscles is:

a.   Troponin . . . . □

b.   Acetylcholine . . . . □

c.   Myosin . . . . □

d.   Serotonin . . . . □

43. Blood leaves the heart from this blood vessel:

a.   Aorta . . . . □

b.   Carotid arteries . . . . □

c.   Cardiac capillaries . . . . □

d.   Circle of Willis . . . . □

44. A motor unit is:

a.   A motor nerve and all the muscle fibers it stimulates . . . . . . □

b.   All the type I and type II fibers in a muscle . . . . □

c.   A single sarcomere. . . . . □

d.   All are correct . . . . □

45. The fiber type that would benefit endurance athletes the most is:

a.   Type I . . . . □

b.   Type Ia . . . . □

    c.   Type IIa . . . . □

    d.   Type IIb . . . . □

46. Which is not considered an anabolic hormone?

    a.   Testosterone . . . . □

    b.   Estrogen. . . . . □

    c.   Cortisol . . . . □

    d.   They are all anabolic. . . . . □

47. Which endocrine gland makes the hormones T3 and T4?

    a.   Liver . . . . □

    b.   Kidney . . . . □

    c.   Thyroid . . . . □

    d.   Adrenal glands . . . . □

48. Which endocrine gland makes the hormone insulin?

    a.   Adrenal glands . . . . □

    b.   Pancreas . . . . □

    c.   Kidney . . . . □

    d.   Liver . . . . □

49. Growth hormone is made in the:

    a.   Kidneys . . . . □

    b.   Adrenal glands . . . . □

    c.   Pituitary gland . . . . □

    d.   Testis . . . . □

50. When ATP loses a phosphate atom, it becomes:

    a.   Cyclic AMP . . . . □

    b.   ADP . . . . □

    c.   Adenosine . . . . □

    d.   GMP . . . . □

51. Women make testosterone:

    a.   True . . . . □

    b.   False. . . . . □

52. Which is most associated with HGH?

    a.   Thyroid hormone . . . . □

a.   IGF . . . . □

b.   Glucagon . . . . □

c.   Acetylcholine . . . . □

53. Which is not a function of muscle tissue?

a.   Heat generation . . . . □

a.   Regulation of blood pressure . . . . □

b.   Breathing . . . . □

c.   They are all functions of muscle tissue. . . . . □

54. The smallest blood vessels in the body are called:

a.   Arterioles . . . . □

a.   Capillaries . . . . □

b.   Venioles . . . . □

c.   Arteries . . . . □

55. An equation for cardiac output is:

a.   Heart rate x stroke volume . . . . □

a.   220 – age . . . . □

b.   Stroke volume x systolic blood pressure . . . . □

c.   Maximum HR – resting HR . . . . □

56. A byproduct of burning carbs anaerobically in glycolysis is:

a.   Carbonic acid . . . . □

a.   Lactate . . . . □

b.   Creatine . . . . □

c.   Lactose . . . . □

57. Which genetic factor plays a role in muscle development?

a.   Muscle fiber type . . . . □

a.   Diabetes . . . . □

b.   Tendon placement . . . . □

c.   Both A and C are correct . . . . □

58. Which energy system lasts approximately 20–30 seconds?

a.   ATP/CP system . . . . □

a.   Glycolysis . . . . □

b.   Phosphagen system . . . . □

   c.   Both A and C are correct . . . . ☐

59. This is not an adaptation to chronic resistance training:

   a.   Increased ATP storage. . . . . ☐

   a.   Increased glycogen storage. . . . . ☐

   b.   Increased bone density . . . . ☐

   c.   All are adaptations. . . . . ☐

60. The heart is contained in:

   a.   Pericardium . . . . ☐

   a.   Bundle of His . . . . ☐

   b.   Fascicle . . . . ☐

   c.   Both A and B are correct . . . . ☐

You've reached the end of this section.

Anatomy and Physiology Section

1. **Blood leaves the heart from which chamber?**

   a. Left atrium . . . . ☐

   b. Right atrium . . . . ☐

   c. Left ventricle . . . . ☐

   d. Right ventricle . . . . ☐

2. **A proprioceptor that detects how much weight is being lifted is:**

   a. Tendon . . . . ☐

   b. Golgi tendon organ . . . . ☐

   c. Myo-tendon. . . . . ☐

   d. None are correct. . . . . ☐

3. **The connective tissue that connects bones together is:**

   a. Tendon . . . . ☐

   b. Ligament . . . . ☐

   c. GTO . . . . ☐

   d. Fascicle . . . . ☐

4. **The "pacemaker" of the heart is found in what chamber?**

   a. Right atrium . . . . ☐

   b. Left atrium . . . . ☐

   c. Right ventricle . . . . ☐

   d. Left ventricle . . . . ☐

5. **Another name for the heart's pacemaker is:**

   a. SA node. . . . . ☐

   b. AV node. . . . . ☐

   c. Pacemaker. . . . . ☐

   d. None are correct. . . . . ☐

6. **The muscle primarily responsible for a movement is called:**

   a. Agonist . . . . ☐

   b. Prime mover . . . . ☐

   c. Synergist . . . . ☐

   d. Both A and B are correct . . . . ☐

7. **When blood leaves the right atrium, it first travels to the:**

   a. Aorta . . . . ☐

b. Lungs . . . . ☐

c. Right ventricle . . . . ☐

d. Left ventricle . . . . ☐

8. **A condition where cartilage between bones is degraded is:**

a. Osteoporosis . . . . ☐

b. Lupus . . . . ☐

c. Osteoarthritis . . . . ☐

d. Fibromyalgia . . . . ☐

9. **The following are functions of cartilage:**

a. Provide smooth surface at joints. . . . . ☐

b. Shock absorption . . . . ☐

c. Helps with muscle-skeletal attachment . . . . ☐

d. All are correct . . . . ☐

10. **In general, blood is carried away from the heart in:**

a. Veins . . . . ☐

b. Arteries . . . . ☐

c. Capillaries . . . . ☐

d. Both A and B are correct . . . . ☐

11. **The iron-carrying compound in red blood cells is called:**

a. Nitric oxide . . . . ☐

b. Erythropoietin . . . . ☐

c. Hemoglobin. . . . . ☐

d. Ribosome . . . . ☐

12. **Which of the following is responsible for removing old or damaged bone?**

a. Osteoblast. . . . . ☐

b. Osteoclast . . . . ☐

c. Fibroblast . . . . ☐

d. Osteocyte . . . . ☐

13. **Where is the hormone insulin produced?**

a. Liver . . . . ☐

b. Pancreas. . . . . ☐

c. Beta cells . . . . ☐

    d.   Both B and C are correct . . . . ☐

14. The number of bones in the adult human skeleton is:

    a.   509 . . . . ☐

    b.   206 . . . . ☐

    c.   311 . . . . ☐

    d.   561 . . . . ☐

15. Growth hormone (HGH) is primarily produced in the:

    a.   Testes . . . . ☐

    b.   Pancreas . . . . ☐

    c.   Brain . . . . ☐

    d.   Muscle . . . . ☐

16. Red blood cells are primarily made in the:

    a.   Erythrocytes. . . . . ☐

    b.   Bone marrow . . . . ☐

    c.   Heart . . . . ☐

    d.   Arteries . . . . ☐

17. Which of the following muscles are used most in the bench press?

    a.   Pectoralis major . . . . ☐

    b.   Anterior deltoids . . . . ☐

    c.   Erector spinae . . . . ☐

    d.   Both A and B are correct . . . . ☐

18. The best overall exercise for reducing fat from behind the arms is:

    a.   Three sets, triceps pushdown (15 reps) . . . . ☐

    b.   Supersets: dips/biceps curls (3 sets/15 reps) . . . . ☐

    c.   Treadmill walking (45 min) . . . . ☐

    d.   Push-ups . . . . ☐

19. Which might be thought to have the greatest percentage of type II muscle fibers?

    a.   Abdominals . . . . ☐

    b.   Buttocks. . . . . ☐

    c.   Soleus . . . . ☐

    d.   Transverse abdominals. . . . . ☐

20. Slow oxidative muscle fibers are also referred to as:

a. Type I . . . . ☐

b. Type IIa . . . . ☐

c. Type IIb . . . . ☐

d. Type IIx . . . . ☐

21. The body's storage form of carbohydrate is:

a. Glucose . . . . ☐

b. Glycogenolysis . . . . ☐

c. Glycogen . . . . ☐

d. Myostarch . . . . ☐

22. Which of the following are muscles of the quadriceps?

a. Vastus intermedius . . . . ☐

b. Biceps femoris . . . . ☐

c. Rectus femoris . . . . ☐

d. Both A and C are correct . . . . ☐

23. Which of the following are muscles of the hamstrings?

a. Biceps femoris . . . . ☐

b. Semimembranosus . . . . ☐

c. Semitendinosus . . . . ☐

d. All are correct . . . . ☐

24. DOMS is caused by:

a. Lactic acid. . . . . ☐

b. Myostatin disruption . . . . ☐

c. Dehydration . . . . ☐

d. None are correct. . . . . ☐

25. Your large upper-arm bone is called the:

a. Femur . . . . ☐

b. Biceps . . . . ☐

c. Humerus . . . . ☐

d. Ulna. . . . . ☐

26. After six months of aerobic training, which would you expect to observe in a client?

a. Increased mitochondria . . . . ☐

b. Increased red blood cells. . . . . ☐

c.   Decreased resting heart rate . . . . □

d.   All are correct . . . . □

27. The term used to describe your hands in a palms-up position is:

a.   Supination . . . . □

b.   Pronation . . . . □

c.   Abduction. . . . . □

d.   Adduction. . . . . □

28. Type II diabetes usually results from:

a.   Lack of the hormone insulin . . . . □

b.   Lack of glutamine . . . . □

c.   Excess calories and lack of exercise . . . . □

d.   An autoimmune disorder . . . . □

29. Carrying excess body fat around the waist increases the risk of:

a.   Arthritis . . . . □

b.   Hamstring tightness . . . . □

c.   Heart disease . . . . □

d.   Low BMI . . . . □

30. 1 MET is equal to which of the following:

a.   2.2 ml O2/KgBW/min . . . . □

b.   3.5 ml O2/KgBW/min . . . . □

c.   Resting VO2 . . . . □

d.   Both B and C are correct . . . . □

31. The nervous system division that increases heart rate is:

a.   Sympathetic NS . . . . □

b.   Parasympathetic NS . . . . □

c.   Proprioceptive NS . . . . □

d.   None are correct. . . . . □

32. Pain in the rotator cuff is localized in what area?

a.   Knee . . . . □

b.   Low back . . . . □

c.   Shoulder . . . . □

d.   Elbow . . . . □

33. This is an example of a weight bearing activity:

    a.   Walking . . . . ☐

    b.   Leg press . . . . ☐

    c.   Lat pulldown . . . . ☐

    d.   Biceps curl . . . . ☐

34. Which is true regarding the effect of estrogen?

    a.   It makes bones weaker. . . . . ☐

    b.   It makes bones stronger . . . . ☐

    c.   Only women make estrogen. . . . . ☐

    d.   Both B and C are correct . . . . ☐

35. The type of cartilage found at the end of bones (e.g., humerus) is:

    a.   Compact bone . . . . ☐

    b.   Articular cartilage . . . . ☐

    c.   Yellow bone marrow. . . . . ☐

    d.   None are correct. . . . . ☐

36. Which resistance would be best for improving bone mineral density?

    a.   45% 10RM . . . . ☐

    b.   65% 15 RM. . . . . ☐

    c.   70% 12RM . . . . ☐

    d.   80% 10RM . . . . ☐

37. Palpating RHR at the neck might do which of the following:

    a.   Raise resting heart rate . . . . ☐

    b.   Lower resting heart rate . . . . ☐

    c.   Decrease anxiety hormones during weight training . . . . ☐

    d.   None are correct. . . . . ☐

38. The proper way to perform the lat pulldown exercise is to:

    a.   Lean back to 45° and pull with arms. . . . . ☐

    b.   Sit up and pull bar behind head, stopping just before bar touches neck . . . . ☐

    c.   Retract shoulder blades and pull to front of head using back muscles . . . . ☐

    d.   Face away from machine; pull bar behind head using arm and shoulders . . . . . . ☐

39. Which is the proper way to do the DB bench press?

    a.   Perform full range of motion, lowering dumbbells until they are level with chest . . ☐

b. Lock out elbows at the top of the range of motion . . . . □

c. The eccentric phase stops when the elbows are at shoulder level . . . . □

d. Do 10 reps with one arm and then 10 with the other . . . . □

40. Which muscle action produces the most DOMS?

a. Isotonic . . . . □

b. Eccentric . . . . □

c. Concentric . . . . □

d. They are all equal . . . . □

41. Which of the following refers to the expansion of blood vessels?

a. Vasoconstriction. . . . . □

b. Vasodilation . . . . □

c. Vasogenesis . . . . □

d. Angiogenesis . . . . □

42. Which best approximates normal blood pH levels?

a. 10 . . . . □

b. 8.5 . . . . □

c. 7.4 . . . . □

d. 1 . . . . □

43. Your client has a hemoglobin A1C level of 9.5. What do you suspect?

a. Rhabdomyolysis. . . . . □

b. Metabolic syndrome. □

c. Heart attack within the past year . . . . □

d. Osteoarthritis . . . . □

44. Which type of cell responds to changes in acidity levels?

a. Proprioceptors. . . . . □

b. Chemoreceptors. . . . . □

c. pH receptors . . . . □

d. Pressure receptors . . . . □

45. The volume of blood pumped from the heart per minute is called:

a. Stroke volume. . . . . □

b. Cardiac output . . . . □

c. Ejection fraction . . . . □

d.   Maximum heart rate . . . . □

46. The adult human body has about how many miles of blood vessels?

a.   10,000 miles . . . . □

b.   30,000 miles . . . . □

c.   45,000 miles . . . . □

d.   100,000 miles . . . . □

47. Which plane divides the body into upper and lower parts?

a.   Frontal . . . . □

b.   Sagittal . . . . □

c.   Transverse . . . . □

d.   Both B and C are correct . . . . □

48. Moving a body part away from the midline is called:

a.   Flexion . . . . □

b.   Abduction. . . . . □

c.   Adduction. . . . . □

d.   Elongation . . . . □

49. Female muscle fibers are different from male muscle fibers.

a.   True . . . . □

b.   False. . . . . □

50. Another name for "FOG" fibers is:

a.   Type I . . . . □

b.   Type Ia . . . . □

c.   Type IIa . . . . □

d.   Type IIb . . . . □

51. Which part of the nervous system increases heart rate?

a.   Sympathetic. . . . . □

b.   Parasympathetic. . . . . □

c.   Automatic. . . . . □

d.   Central . . . . □

52. Another name for oxidative fibers is:

a.   Type I fibers . . . . □

b.   Type IIa fibers . . . . □

    c.   Type II fibers . . . . ☐

    d.   None are correct. . . . . ☐

53. When two bones come together, it is called a:

    a.   Synapse . . . . ☐

    b.   Joint. . . . . ☐

    c.   Ball and socket . . . . ☐

    d.   Junction . . . . ☐

54. Which muscle action is not normally produced?

    a.   Isotonic . . . . ☐

    b.   Isokinetic . . . . ☐

    c.   Concentric . . . . ☐

    d.   Eccentric . . . . ☐

55. The percentage of blood pumped from the heart per heartbeat is:

    a.   Cardiac output . . . . ☐

    b.   Ejection fraction . . . . ☐

    c.   Stroke volume. . . . . ☐

    d.   None are correct. . . . . ☐

56. Which is a symptom of metabolic syndrome?

    a.   Abdominal obesity . . . . ☐

    b.   Increased blood pressure. . . . . ☐

    c.   Increased HDL . . . . ☐

    d.   Only A and B are correct . . . . ☐

57. The blood in the heart after the filling phase is called:

    a.   End systolic volume . . . . ☐

    b.   End diastolic volume . . . . ☐

    c.   Residual volume. . . . . ☐

    d.   Ejection fraction . . . . ☐

58. Muscles are connected to bones via:

    a.   Tendons. . . . . ☐

    b.   Ligaments . . . . ☐

    c.   Muscles . . . . ☐

    d.   Both A and C are correct . . . . ☐

59. Which statement about skeletal muscles is true?

    a.   Muscles can only pull . . . . □

    b.   Muscles can only push . . . . □

60. Muscle fibers are composed of smaller units called:

    a.   Fasciculi . . . . □

    b.   Myofibril . . . . □

    c.   Endomysium . . . . □

    d.   None are correct. . . . . □

You've reached the end of this section.

Fitness Testing Section

1. **The "core" consists of which muscle group(s)?**

   a. Abdominals . . . . ☐

   b. Glutes . . . . ☐

   c. Back musculature . . . . ☐

   d. All are correct . . . . ☐

2. **If a person is using the treadmill at 10 METs, what is their VO2?**

   a. 10 . . . . ☐

   b. 35 . . . . ☐

   c. 50 . . . . ☐

   d. Cannot be determined . . . . ☐

3. **Which are desirable waist circumferences in men and women?**

   a. Men < 40 inches; women < 35 inches . . . . ☐

   b. Men > 40 inches; women > 35 inches . . . . ☐

   c. Men < 30 inches; women < 15 inches . . . . ☐

   d. Men > 45 inches; women > 35 inches . . . . ☐

4. **Which is the heaviest resistance?**

   a. 1 RM . . . . ☐

   b. 10RM . . . . ☐

   c. 15 RM . . . . ☐

   d. 20 RM . . . . ☐

5. **Which is a test of CV endurance?**

   a. BIA . . . . ☐

   b. Jumping jacks . . . . ☐

   c. Timed push ups . . . . ☐

   d. None are correct. . . . . ☐

6. **Which of the following is the best general warm-up exercise?**

   a. Two sets, 40% 10 RM bench press . . . . ☐

   b. Stretch, five minutes. . . . . ☐

   c. Elliptical, ten minutes . . . . ☐

   d. One set, 60% 10 RM bench press . . . . ☐

7. **Stretching for thirty minutes prior to exercise has the potential to cause a(n):**

   a. Increase in muscle power . . . . ☐

b.   Decrease in muscle power . . . . ☐

c.   Increase in blood sugar levels . . . . ☐

d.   Increase in core strength . . . . ☐

8.   **An example of a fitness "field test" is:**

a.   One RM bench press . . . . ☐

b.   1.5 mile run . . . . ☐

c.   Timed sit-ups . . . . ☐

d.   Three minute step test . . . . ☐

9.   **Which of the following constitutes a normal BMI?**

a.   Under 18.5 . . . . ☐

b.   18.5–24.9 . . . . ☐

c.   25.0–29.9 . . . . ☐

d.   Above 30 . . . . ☐

10. **Which of the following can alter BIA results?**

a.   Working out just prior to the test . . . . ☐

b.   Working out just after the test . . . . ☐

c.   Not urinating before the test . . . . ☐

d.   All are correct . . . . ☐

11. **Which of the following is true about high density lipoprotein (HDL)?**

a.   Desirable > 45 . . . . ☐

b.   It's the bad cholesterol . . . . ☐

c.   Desirable < 15 . . . . ☐

d.   Desirable < 20 . . . . ☐

12. **Using air-displacement plethysmography measures:**

a.   Cardiovascular fitness . . . . ☐

b.   Body fat . . . . ☐

c.   Muscle endurance . . . . ☐

d.   Bone density . . . . ☐

13. **Blood pressure of 120/80 mm Hg is referred to as:**

a.   Normal . . . . ☐

b.   Low normal . . . . ☐

c.   Prehypertension . . . . ☐

d. Hypotension . . . . ☐

14. Your client's RHR is 105 bpm. This is called:

a. Bradycardia . . . . ☐

b. Tachycardia . . . . ☐

c. Ventricular fibrillation. . . . . ☐

d. Hypercardia . . . . ☐

15. The average resting heart rate for a healthy adult is:

a. 100–120 bpm . . . . ☐

b. 60–80 bpm . . . . ☐

c. 60–100 bpm . . . . ☐

d. 60–70 bpm . . . . ☐

16. The best place to measure a pulse on another person is the:

a. Right side of the neck . . . . ☐

b. Thumb side of the wrist . . . . ☐

c. Pinky finger side of the wrist . . . . ☐

d. Left side of the neck. . . . . ☐

17. Which body composition method is the most accurate?

a. Bioelectric impedance analysis. . . . . ☐

b. Hydrostatic weighing . . . . ☐

c. Near-infrared interactance. . . . . ☐

d. Skinfold calipers. . . . . ☐

18. When using a skinfold caliper, which statement is correct?

a. Most accurate in post-menopausal women . . . ☐

b. Most accurate in young athletes (12–17 years of age) . . . ☐

c. Less accurate than hand-held BIA devices . . . . ☐

d. None are correct. . . . . ☐

19. Who should not undergo bioelectric impedance analysis?

a. Pregnant women . . . . ☐

b. People with pacemakers . . . . ☐

c. Children (13–17 years of age) . . . . ☐

d. Both A and B are correct . . . . ☐

20. Bioelectric impedance analysis may yield inaccurate results in:

a.   Overweight people . . . . ☐

b.   Underweight people . . . . ☐

c.   In people with osteoporosis . . . . ☐

d.   Both A and B are correct . . . . ☐

21. In exercise, the letters RM stand for:

a.   Reps per minute . . . . ☐

b.   Rhabdomyolysis muscle . . . . ☐

c.   Repetition maximum . . . . ☐

d.   Rate of maximum exertion . . . . ☐

22. Timed push-ups are a common test of which fitness component:

a.   Muscle strength . . . . ☐

b.   Muscle endurance . . . . ☐

c.   Muscle power . . . . ☐

d.   Core strength . . . . ☐

23. Exercise at 5 METs is similar to which of the following?

a.   Metabolic rate is five times higher than resting rate . . . . ☐

b.   Calorie usage is five times lower than resting rate . . . . ☐

c.   VO2 max is five times higher than normal . . . . ☐

d.   Both A and B are correct . . . . ☐

24. Which is the starting point for hypertension?

a.   150/70 . . . . ☐

b.   120/80 . . . . ☐

c.   140/90 . . . . ☐

d.   130/80 . . . . ☐

25. Before taking resting heart rate (RHR), which is recommended?

a.   Sit quietly for 5–10 minutes . . . . ☐

b.   Determine max HR first . . . . ☐

c.   Take blood pressure first . . . . ☐

d.   Both A and B are correct . . . . ☐

26. A low resting heart rate (e.g., less than 60 bpm) in someone who does not exercise regularly may be a sign of:

a.   A caffeine-free diet . . . . ☐

b.   Low physical fitness level . . . . ☐

c. Recently smoking cessation ☐
d. Blood pressure medication use ☐

27. Crunches and sit-ups are contraindicated in which of the following conditions?

a. Brest cancer ☐
b. Diabetes. ☐
c. Children under the age of twelve ☐
d. Osteoporosis ☐

28. A BMI of 30 may indicate:

a. Low RHR ☐
b. High fitness level ☐
c. Obesity ☐
d. Blood pressure medication use ☐

29. Systolic blood pressure:

a. Decreases as exercise gets harder ☐
b. Is the top number of the blood pressure fraction ☐
c. Is the bottom number of the blood pressure fraction ☐
d. Both A and B are correct ☐

30. VO2 max is best defined as a measurement of:

a. Muscular power ☐
b. Aerobic fitness ☐
c. Body mass index ☐
d. Bone mineral density ☐

31. Which is not a body composition test?

a. Air plethysmography ☐
b. DEXA ☐
c. Body Mass Index ☐
d. All are body fat tests ☐

32. Which of the following can be a sign of a heart attack in process?

a. Jaw pain ☐
b. Vomiting ☐
c. Chest pain ☐
d. All are correct ☐

33. A one-page form that identifies those needing medical clearance is a:

    a.   Waiver . . . . □

    b.   Health history form . . . . □

    c.   PAR Q . . . . □

    d.   None are correct. . . . . □

34. Which might you expect to see in a bodybuilder?

    a.   High RHR . . . . □

    b.   High BMI. . . . . □

    c.   Very high VO2 max (above 60) . . . . □

    d.   Decreased capillary density . . . . □

35. When performing skinfold testing, which is necessary?

    a.   Take measurements from the right side of the body only . . . . □

    b.   Take measurements from the left side of the body only . . . . □

    c.   Take measurements from both sides of the body . . . . □

    d.   Take the average of both right and left side measurements. . . . . □

36. Which medical acronym indicates a heart attack?

    a.   MI . . . . □

    b.   HTN . . . . □

    c.   CHD . . . . □

    d.   None are correct. . . . . □

37. The medical acronym CAD refers to:

    a.   High blood pressure. . . . . □

    b.   Cardiac advanced diabetes. . . . . □

    c.   Heart disease . . . . □

    d.   Cleared for daily activity . . . . □

38. Your client's mother had a heart attack at age sixty-three. What do you recommend?

    a.   Interval training to boost HDL . . . . □

    b.   Circuit training, 20 RM resistance . . . . □

    c.   Medical clearance . . . . □

    d.   Fish oil supplements. . . . . □

39. A client who writes "HTN" on his health form is telling you that he has:

    a.   Hypothyroidism. . . . . □

b. Hypertension . . . . ☐

c. High cholesterol. . . . . ☐

d. Hyperthyroidism . . . . ☐

40. An advantage of the Borg Scale (6–20 version) is:

a. Estimates exercise HR. . . . . ☐

b. Estimates exercise BP . . . . ☐

c. Estimates resting heart rate . . . . ☐

d. Both A and B are correct . . . . ☐

41. The word "contraindication" means:

a. Formally accepted treatment option. . . . . ☐

b. Avoid because of side effects. . . . . ☐

c. Side-effect free. . . . . ☐

d. None are correct. . . . . ☐

42. When should a RHR be taken?

a. Upon waking up in the morning . . . . ☐

b. After sitting quietly for 5–10 minutes . . . . ☐

c. At the end of the night, before bed . . . . ☐

d. Both A and B are correct . . . . ☐

43. During testing, your fifty-year-old client complains of fatigue. What should you do?

a. Give them verbal encouragement to continue . . . . ☐

b. Use the RPE scale . . . . ☐

c. Stop the test. . . . . ☐

d. Let them sip water during the test. . . . . ☐

44. A possible drawback to testing during the first week of training may be:

a. Greater risk of injury . . . . ☐

b. More DOMS . . . . ☐

c. Inaccuracy of the results. . . . . ☐

d. None are correct. . . . . ☐

45. In general, which form should not be completed by a seventeen-year-old client?

a. PAR Q . . . . ☐

b. Waiver . . . . ☐

c. Health history form . . . . ☐

    d.   Both A and C are correct . . . . ☐

46. Having very flexible joints is termed:

    a.   Agonist-antagonist imbalance . . . . ☐

    b.   Laxity . . . . ☐

    c.   Hypo-flexibility . . . . ☐

    d.   None are correct. . . . . ☐

47. When determining if a fitness test is appropriate, what should the trainer consider?

    a.   If the test measures what it's supposed to measure. . . . . ☐

    b.   If the test will exacerbate preexisting injuries of the client . . . . ☐

    c.   If the test will embarrass the client . . . . ☐

    d.   All are correct . . . . ☐

48. Timed sit-ups measure:

    a.   Cardiovascular endurance . . . . ☐

    b.   Local muscle endurance . . . . ☐

    c.   Total body muscle endurance . . . . ☐

    d.   Core strength . . . . ☐

49. The T Test is designed to measure:

    a.   Cardiovascular endurance . . . . ☐

    b.   Agility. . . . . ☐

    c.   Power . . . . ☐

    d.   Muscle endurance . . . . ☐

50. Your seventy-year-old client complains of fast-acting calf pain when walking. The pain subsides quickly after she sits down. What might you suspect?

    a.   Rheumatoid arthritis . . . . ☐

    b.   Osteoarthritis . . . . ☐

    c.   Atherosclerosis . . . . ☐

    d.   She is a beginner with a low fitness level. . . . . ☐

51. A drawback to skinfold testing can include:

    a.   Embarrassing the client . . . . ☐

    b.   Sexual harassment allegations . . . . ☐

    c.   Inaccurate results in morbidly obese populations . . . . ☐

    d.   All of the above . . . . ☐

52. You notice that the skin behind the neck of your African-American client is darker

than at other areas of the body. You suspect:

a. Rhabdomyolysis. . . . . ☐

b. Insulin resistance . . . . ☐

c. Hypertension . . . . ☐

d. Dehydration . . . . ☐

53. When should waist circumference measurement be taken?

a. After they suck in their belly . . . . . . ☐

b. After they forcefully exhale . . . . ☐

c. After the warm-up exercise . . . . ☐

d. After a normal exhalation . . . . ☐

54. Which can contribute to error when taking blood pressure?

a. Using the wrong size cuff . . . . ☐

b. Taking BP after physical activity . . . ☐

c. Recent smoking by the client . . . . . . ☐

d. All are correct . . . . ☐

55. Which should occur at the first meeting with a new client?

a. Creation of weight loss eating programs . . . ☐

b. Discussion of goals . . . . ☐

c. Determining compatibility . . . . ☐

d. Both B and C are correct . . . . ☐

56. Trainer liability insurance may not protect against:

a. Sexual harassment . . . . ☐

b. Dietary supplement recommendations . . . ☐

c. Diet plan creation . . . . ☐

d. All of the above . . . . ☐

57. The treadmill five-minute fitness test is designed to measure:

a. Muscle endurance . . . . ☐

b. Cardiovascular endurance . . . . ☐

c. Maximal heart rate . . . . ☐

d. Both A and B are correct . . . . ☐

58. The hand-held dynamometer test is designed to measure:

a. Total body strength . . . . ☐

b. Grip strength . . . . □

c. Total body power . . . . □

d. Grip endurance . . . . □

59. The faster the heart rate returns to normal after exercise:

a. The greater the risk of heart disease . . . . □

b. The poorer the fitness level . . . . □

c. The greater the fitness level . . . . □

d. Has no relationship to health or fitness . . . . □

60. A VO2 max of 39 ml O2/kg/min corresponds to what MET level?

a. 39 . . . . □

b. 11 . . . . □

c. 15 . . . . □

d. 29.5 . . . . □

You've reached the end of this section.

Exercise Program Design Section

1. **Altering exercise frequency, intensity, sets, reps, and rest periods throughout a training program is called:**

    a. Cycling . . . . ☐

    b. Periodization . . . . ☐

    c. Cross cycling . . . . ☐

    d. Interval training . . . . ☐

2. **Which of the following should be developed first in a healthy beginner?**

    a. Muscle strength . . . . ☐

    b. Muscle endurance . . . . ☐

    c. Muscle hypertrophy . . . . ☐

    d. Reduction in body fat . . . . ☐

3. **Which is best for reducing belly fat?**

    a. 50 crunches, 5 days/week . . . . ☐

    b. 25 sit-ups, 3 days/week . . . . ☐

    c. Interval training, 3 days/week, 20 min . . . . ☐

    d. Treadmill, 4 days/week, 40 min . . . . ☐

4. **Your client wants to reduce the fat under her arms. The best routine is:**

    a. Triceps extension: 4 sets of 12–20 reps, 4 days/week . . . . ☐

    b. Triceps extension and kickbacks: 4 sets each, 20 reps, 4 days/week . . . . ☐

    c. 3 sets of 10 RM squats; then, 2 sets each: bench press, dips, kickbacks . . . . . . ☐

    d. None are correct. . . . . ☐

5. **Which is the best overall order of progression to train a client?**

    a. Strength, hypertrophy, power, endurance . . . . ☐

    b. Hypertrophy, strength, power, endurance . . . . ☐

    c. Endurance, hypertrophy, strength, power . . . . ☐

    d. Body comp, power, hypertrophy, strength . . . . ☐

6. **Which should be used with caution in those with high blood pressure?**

    a. 1 RM bench press . . . . ☐

    b. Seated shoulder press . . . . ☐

    c. Lat pulldown . . . . ☐

    d. Both A and B are correct . . . . ☐

7. **Which of the following constitutes a superset?**

a. Leg press/calf raise. . . . . ☐

b. Lat pulldown/bench press . . . . ☐

c. Both A and B . . . . ☐

d. None are correct. . . . . ☐

8. Which is the most logical order of exercises?

a. Shoulder press, bench press, leg press, biceps curls . . . . ☐

b. Leg press, shoulder press, bench press, calf raise . . . . ☐

c. Bench press, lat pulldown, leg press, hamstring curl . . . . ☐

d. Dips, shoulder press, lateral raise, bench press . . . . ☐

9. The best aerobic exercise prescription for general health is to work out:

a. 3 days/week . . . . ☐

b. 4 days/week . . . . ☐

c. 5–6 days/week. . . . . ☐

d. 6–7 days/week. . . . . ☐

10. For general health, how many days each week should strength training be performed?

a. 1 day/week . . . . ☐

b. 2 days/week . . . . ☐

c. 2–3 days/week. . . . . ☐

d. 4–5 days/week. . . . . ☐

11. About how long does it take for atrophy to occur in healthy people?

a. 1 week. . . . . ☐

b. 2–3 weeks . . . . ☐

c. 3–4 weeks . . . . ☐

d. 4–6 weeks . . . . ☐

12. The FITT principle consists of all of the following except:

a. Frequency of exercise . . . . ☐

b. Duration of exercise. . . . . ☐

c. Termination of exercise . . . . ☐

d. Type of exercise . . . . ☐

13. Which of the following represents the RPE scale?

a. 0–10 scale . . . . ☐

b. 6–20 scale . . . . ☐

c.   1–12 scale . . . . □

d.   Both A and B are correct . . . . □

14. 80% Karvonen Hr max is most similar to which of the following?

a.   80% max blood pressure . . . . □

b.   80% resting heart rate. . . . . □

c.   80% percent of VO2 max . . . . □

d.   Rating of 6 on the RPE scale . . . . □

15. A healthy, person wants to run a half marathon six months from today. Which is the best overall training program?

a.   Circuit training (50% 1RM, 25 seconds rest between sets) . . . . □

b.   Plyometrics coupled with circuit training . . . . □

c.   Running. . . . . □

d.   Weight lifting (80% 10 RM, 3 sets, 30 seconds rest between sets). . . . . □

16. What rest period between sets is best for improving muscular endurance?

a.   30 sec–1 min . . . . □

b.   < 30 sec . . . . □

c.   1.5min–2 min. . . . . □

d.   1 min exactly . . . . □

17. A person lifting weights at 80% 10 RM takes rest periods of 90 seconds between sets. What is the most likely goal of her training program?

a.   Muscular endurance. □

b.   Cardiovascular endurance . . . . □

c.   Muscle hypertrophy. □

d.   Muscular power. . . . . □

18. Volume of exercise is calculated by which of the following formulas?

a.   Blood pressure x heart rate . . . . □

b.   Reps x sets x weight . . . . □

c.   Max heart rate – resting heart rate. . . . . □

d.   Max blood pressure – resting blood pressure . . . . □

19. The higher the RM, the heavier the resistance.

a.   True . . . . □

b.   False. . . . . □

20. A client is taking meds for hypertension. Which would be the best way to monitor

exercise intensity?

   a. Karvonen heart rate . . . . ☐

   b. 60%–70% Max HR. . . . . ☐

   c. Use the "fat burn" program on the treadmill . . . . ☐

   d. RPE scale . . . . ☐

21. When in doubt, which program is safest for special populations?

   a. Pyramid sets. . . . . ☐

   b. Circuit training . . . . ☐

   c. Super sets . . . . ☐

   d. Interval training . . . . ☐

22. What is the correct sequence of the Karvonen heart-rate formula?

   a. 220 – age x percent of desired heart rate. . . . . ☐

   b. 220 – age – RHR x percent of desired heart rate + RHR . . ☐

   c. 206 – age – RHR x percent of desired heart rate + RHR . . ☐

   d. 220 + age – RHR + 3.5 x percent of desired heart rate + RHR . . ☐

23. What is the estimated maximum heart rate of a fifty-year-old man?

   a. 165 bpm . . . . ☐

   b. 220 bpm . . . . ☐

   c. 170 bpm . . . . ☐

   d. 200 bpm . . . . ☐

24. The RHR of your client is 50 bpm. What might account for this?

   a. He is healthy; works out. . . . . ☐

   b. He is healthy; doesn't work out . . . . ☐

   c. Blood pressure medication usage . . . . ☐

   d. Both A and C are correct . . . . ☐

25. Using the Karvonen formula, calculate 60% and 80% max HR for a thirty-year-old woman who has an RHR of 60 bpm:

   a. 138–164 bpm . . . . ☐

   b. 127–167 bpm . . . . ☐

   c. 76–101 bpm . . . . ☐

   d. 60–100 bpm . . . . ☐

26. The seated calf raise works primarily which muscle?

a. Gastrocnemius . . . . ☐

b. Tibialis anterior . . . . ☐

c. Soleus . . . . ☐

d. Extensor carpi ulnaris . . . . ☐

27. Which is the best option for improving bone density?

a. Swimming. . . . . ☐

b. Interval training . . . . ☐

c. Leg-extension machine . . . . ☐

d. Leg-press machine

28. Which of the following is a compound exercise?

a. Seated leg press . . . . ☐

b. Standing biceps curl with dumbbells . . . . ☐

c. Seated leg-extension machine . . . . ☐

d. Standing triceps push down . . . . ☐

29. Which of the following is a closed-chain exercise?

a. Leg extension . . . . ☐

b. Leg curl . . . . ☐

c. Leg press . . . . ☐

d. Both A and B are correct . . . . ☐

30. Hammer curls work this muscle group the most:

a. Hamstrings . . . . ☐

b. Latissimus dorsi . . . . ☐

c. Brachialis . . . . ☐

d. Biceps . . . . ☐

31. Proprioceptive neuromuscular facilitation (PNF) helps improve:

a. Flexibility . . . . ☐

b. VO2 max . . . . ☐

c. 1RM bench press . . . . ☐

d. Muscle endurance . . . . ☐

32. Your client is a tennis player. Before her game, you recommend:

a. Stretch, then warm up. . . . . ☐

b. Warm up, then stretch . . . . ☐

c.   Circuit training, warm up, stretch. . . . . ☐

d.   Only stretch. . . . . ☐

33. Before bench pressing, which is an example of a dynamic warm up?

a.   PNF. . . . . ☐

b.   Bench press at 40% 10 RM . . . . ☐

c.   Bench press at 95% 10 RM . . . . ☐

d.   Lat pulldown 50% 1RM . . . . ☐

34. The best grip when spotting the bench press is:

a.   Supinated grip. . . . . ☐

b.   Pronated grip . . . . ☐

c.   Alternated grip . . . . ☐

d.   Spot at the elbows . . . . ☐

35. A common error during the seated row is:

a.   Bending forward at the hips/lower back during the eccentric phase . . . . ☐

b.   Curling the wrists inward during the pulling phase . . . . ☐

c.   Not retracting the shoulder blades. . . . . ☐

d.   All are correct . . . . ☐

36. The main muscles used during the lat pulldown include:

a.   Rhomboids . . . . ☐

b.   Posterior deltoids . . . . ☐

c.   Triceps . . . . ☐

d.   Both A and B are correct . . . . ☐

37. In periodization, this is not a phase of the Preparatory Period:

a.   Hypertrophy . . . . ☐

b.   Strength. . . . . ☐

c.   Body composition. . . . . ☐

d.   Power . . . . ☐

38. A possible drawback to the supine leg curl machine might be:

a.   Works the calves too much . . . . ☐

b.   Decrease in BP when getting up. . . . . ☐

c.   Only works biceps femoris . . . . ☐

d.   All are correct . . . . ☐

39. When exercising in the water, which is true?

    a.   Less DOMS. . . . . ☐

    b.   Greater bone mineral density . . . . ☐

    c.   More DOMS . . . . ☐

    d.   Less balance is required . . . . ☐

40. When performing the bench press, which is correct?

    a.   Lift the buttocks off the bench during the concentric phase . . . . ☐

    b.   Press the head into the bench during the concentric phase . . . . ☐

    c.   The wrists should be bent during the bench press . . . . ☐

    d.   None are correct. . . . . ☐

41. Which is true about strength testing?

    a.   It is dependent on the muscle tested. . . . . ☐

    b.   One test provides total body strength results . . . . ☐

    c.   Speed of movement should be considered . . . . ☐

    d.   Both A and C are correct . . . . ☐

42. Which exercise sequence is most logical?

    a.   Leg press, chest press, lat pulldown, shoulder press . . . . ☐

    b.   Chest press, incline press, decline press, push-ups . . . . ☐

    c.   Leg press, squat, leg extension, leg curl . . . . ☐

    d.   Pull-ups, lat pulldown, biceps curl, hammer curls . . . . ☐

43. Your new client had a heart attack three months ago. You recommend:

    a.   Complete health history form; interval training three times per week . . . . ☐

    b.   Complete waiver; perform circuits and interval training two to three times per week ☐

    c.   Obtain medical clearance from attending physician first . . . . ☐

    d.   Train them and advise physician oversight. . . . . ☐

44. Your client just had heart attack in the gym. What should you do?

    a.   Call 911

    b.   Perform CPR/AED until help arrives . . . . ☐

    c.   Make him comfortable until paramedics arrive . . . . ☐

    d.   Both A and C are correct . . . . ☐

45. Which should be considered for 1 RM testing?

    a.   Age of client. . . . . ☐

b.   Medical conditions . . . . ☐

c.   Preexisting injuries . . . . ☐

d.   All are correct . . . . ☐

46.   Your client gives you a doctor slip stating "improve BMD." This refers to:

a.   Muscles . . . . ☐

b.   Activities of daily living . . . . ☐

c.   Bones . . . . ☐

d.   Blood pressure. . . . . ☐

47.   Which is true about compound exercises?

a.   Greater muscle activation . . . . ☐

b.   They are multi-joint activities . . . . ☐

c.   They improve BMD. . . . . ☐

d.   All are correct . . . . ☐

48.   Which percent of 1 RM is most appropriate for muscle hypertrophy?

a.   90%–100% . . . . ☐

b.   60%–80% . . . . ☐

c.   40%–45% . . . . ☐

d.   30%–40% . . . . ☐

49.   Which of the following would be the safest progression?

a.   Increase reps performed before increasing amount of weight lifted . . . . ☐

b.   Increase sets performed before increasing reps performed . . . . ☐

c.   Increase weight lifted before increasing sets performed . . . . ☐

d.   None are correct. . . . . ☐

50.   Your client has arthritis. Which is the best overall program?

a.   Interval training . . . . ☐

b.   Split routine. . . . . ☐

c.   Circuit training . . . . ☐

d.   Drop sets . . . . ☐

51.   The condition best described as an autoimmune disorder is:

a.   Osteoarthritis . . . . ☐

b.   Rheumatoid arthritis . . . . ☐

c.   High blood pressure. . . . . ☐

d. Fibromyalgia . . . . ☐

52. Which is not an accepted principle of exercise?

a. FITT principle . . . . ☐

b. SAID principle . . . . ☐

c. Reversibility principle . . . . ☐

d. All are accepted principles . . . . ☐

53. A drawback to using the RPE scale is:

a. It doesn't work with older adults . . . . ☐

b. People must be familiar with what the numbers represent . . . . . . ☐

c. It only estimates maximum heart rate . . . . ☐

d. All are drawbacks to using the RPE scale . . . . ☐

54. The acronym "OBLA" is most often associated with:

a. Strength training . . . . ☐

b. Water aerobics. . . . . ☐

c. Lactate accumulation . . . . ☐

d. The point of greatest fat burning during exercise . . . . ☐

55. Which duration on the treadmill—to reach over time—is most appropriate for weight loss?

a. 15 minutes . . . . ☐

b. 30 minutes . . . . ☐

c. 45 minutes . . . . ☐

d. 60 minutes . . . . ☐

56. Which exercise program is specifically designed to improve muscular power?

a. Plyometrics . . . . ☐

b. Super slow. . . . . ☐

c. Super sets . . . . ☐

d. HITT . . . . ☐

57. A physical therapist advises you that your new client has weak biceps femoris muscles. The exercise that will strengthen this muscle is:

a. Bench press . . . . ☐

b. Biceps curls with straight bar . . . . ☐

c. Leg-curl machine . . . . ☐

d. Leg-extension machine . . . . ☐

58. Your client has a blood pressure of 300/115. How to you advise him?

    a.   Eat something; return to the gym later in the day to workout . . . . ☐

    b.   Do interval training for twenty minutes; recheck blood pressure . . . . ☐

    c.   See doctor before returning to exercise . . . . ☐

    d.   Exercise as usual, but continually ask him how he feels . . . . ☐

59. Which would be an appropriate fitness test for a morbidly obese client?

    a.   Timed sit-ups . . . . ☐

    b.   Timed push-ups. . . . . ☐

    c.   1.5 run/walk test . . . . ☐

    d.   None of the above. . . . . ☐

60. Which exercise would be most appropriate for helping sarcopenia?

    a.   Water aerobics. . . . . ☐

    b.   Leg press . . . . ☐

    c.   Elliptical . . . . ☐

    d.   Standing calf raises . . . . ☐

You've reached the end of this section.

Nutrition and Sports Nutrition Section

1. **How many calories are in a gram of protein, carbohydrate, and fat?**

   a. 4, 4, and 9 respectively . . . . □

   b. 4, 5, and 10 respectively. □

   c. 4, 5, and 6 respectively . . . . □

   d. 8, 9, and 10 respectively. □

2. **A life-threatening condition from drinking too much water is called:**

   a. Hyperosmosis . . . . □

   b. Hyponatremia. . . . . □

   c. Ketoacidosis. . . . . □

   d. Metabolic hydrosis . . . . □

3. **How many grams are in one ounce?**

   a. 4 . . . . □

   b. 28 . . . . □

   c. 10 . . . . □

   d. 3.5 . . . . □

4. **How many calories do B vitamins contain?**

   a. 10 . . . . □

   b. 3 . . . . □

   c. 0 . . . . □

   d. 2.2 . . . . □

5. **The RDA for protein for a healthy sedentary adult is approximately:**

   a. 0.4 g/lb . . . . □

   b. 1 g /lb . . . . □

   c. 2 g/lb . . . . □

   d. 1.2 g/lb . . . . □

6. **A common side effect of creatine supplements is:**

   a. Liver problems . . . . □

   b. Kidney problems . . . . □

   c. Muscle cramping . . . . □

   d. None are correct. . . . . □

7. **As exercise intensity increases, humans burn more:**

   a. Fat . . . . □

b.   Carbohydrate . . . . ☐

c.   Protein . . . . ☐

d.   All are used the same . . . . ☐

8.   The average adult has enough glycogen to run approximately:

a.   5 miles . . . . ☐

b.   10 miles . . . . ☐

c.   20 miles . . . . ☐

d.   40 miles . . . . ☐

9.   You're asked which supplement helps weight loss the most. You answer:

a.   Yohimbe. . . . . ☐

b.   Raspberry ketones. . . . . ☐

c.   Citrus aurantium . . . . ☐

d.   None are correct. . . . . ☐

10.   The type of creatine that has been studied most by researchers is:

a.   Buffered creatine . . . . ☐

b.   Creatine monohydrate . . . . ☐

c.   Micronized creatine . . . . ☐

d.   Creatine combined with glutamine . . . . ☐

11.   About what percent of fats should be consumed as part of a healthy diet?

a.   Less than 10% . . . . ☐

b.   Less than 20% . . . . ☐

c.   Less than 30% . . . . ☐

d.   Between 10% and 20% . . . . ☐

12.   A healthy person works out three times and asks how much protein he needs. Which is most appropriate?

a.   1 gram per pound . . . . ☐

b.   0.4 grams per pound . . . . ☐

c.   1 to 2.2 grams per pound . . . . ☐

d.   0.6–0.9 grams per pound . . . . ☐

13.   The letters RDA stand for:

a.   Recommended daily allowance . . . . ☐

b.   Recommended dietary allowance . . . . ☐

c.   Registered dietitian allowed . . . . ☐

    d.   Readily daily allowance . . . . □

14. What are the fat soluble vitamins?

    a.   All of the B vitamins . . . . □

    b.   Vitamins E, A, D and K. . . . . □

    c.   Vitamins A, B12, C and D . . . . □

    d.   Vitamins C and D . . . . □

15. Glutamine is an example of a(n):

    a.   Essential amino acid. . . . . □

    b.   Non-essential amino acid . . . . □

    c.   Protein . . . . □

    d.   Probiotic . . . . □

16. Which of the following are branch chain amino acids (BCAA)?

    a.   Leucine, isoleucine, valine. □

    b.   Glutamine, arginine, leucine . . . . □

    c.   Myostatin, glutamine, homocysteine . . . . □

    d.   Lysine, glutamine, arginine . . . . □

17. Humans can only absorb thirty-five to forty grams of protein per meal.

    a.   True . . . . □

    b.   False. . . . . □

18. How many calories are in one pound of fat?

    a.   9 . . . . □

    b.   2.2 . . . . □

    c.   3500 . . . . □

    d.   2250 . . . . □

19. Which fats have the most calories?

    a.   Trans fats . . . . □

    b.   Saturated fats . . . . □

    c.   Monounsaturated fats . . . . □

    d.   None are correct. . . . . □

20. Short-term weight loss from low carb diets is primarily due to:

    a.   Fat loss . . . . □

    b.   Water loss . . . . □

    c.   Muscle loss . . . . ☐

    d.   Vitamin and fat loss . . . . ☐

21. Which amount of protein might be best for a runner?

    a.   1 g/lb . . . . ☐

    b.   0.4 g/lb . . . . ☐

    c.   0.6 g/lb . . . . ☐

    d.   0.9 g/lb . . . . ☐

22. Which is true about dietary supplements?

    a.   The FDA tests supplements . . . . ☐

    b.   Supplements are regulated. . . . . ☐

    c.   Companies can use any ingredients they want. . . . . ☐

    d.   Supplements are not regulated . . . . ☐

23. Which does not contain significant amounts of creatine?

    a.   Swordfish . . . . ☐

    b.   Turkey. . . . . ☐

    c.   Salmon . . . . ☐

    d.   Glutamine. . . . . ☐

24. The fiber type expected to have the most creatine content is:

    a.   Type I . . . . ☐

    b.   Type IIa . . . . ☐

    c.   Type IIb . . . . ☐

    d.   They all have equal amounts . . . . ☐

25. Which is true concerting the use of ergogenic aids?

    a.   They help arthritis. . . . . ☐

    b.   They are said to improve exercise performance . . . . ☐

    c.   They reduce blood pressure . . . . ☐

    d.   None are correct. . . . . ☐

26. Which individual might be helped to most by glutamine supplements?

    a.   A marathon runner . . . . ☐

    b.   A healthy fifty-year-old man who lifts weights four days a week (1 hr/day) . . . . . ☐

    c.   A healthy twenty-five-year-old woman who is just starting to working out . . . . . ☐

    d.   None are correct. . . . . ☐

27. Which of the following is an essential amino acid?

 a. Tryptophan . . . . □

 b. Valine . . . . □

 c. Leucine . . . . □

 d. All are correct . . . . □

28. Which of the following is not a vitamin?

 a. Beta carotene . . . . □

 b. Folate . . . . □

 c. Riboflavin . . . . □

 d. Niacin . . . . □

29. Which of the following best represents the RDA for fiber?

 a. 5–10 g . . . . □

 b. 10–20 g . . . . □

 c. 20–30 g . . . . □

 d. 40–50 g . . . . □

30. Which statement is true concerning vitamins?

 a. They are made in the body . . . . □

 b. They are not made in the body . . . . □

 c. They provide extra energy ("pep") . . . . □

 d. Only B and C are correct . . . . □

31. In the course of a day, which results in the most calories being used?

 a. RMR . . . . □

 b. Exercise . . . . □

 c. Thermic effect of food/digestion . . . . □

 d. None of the answers are correct . . . . □

32. A diet often recommended to people with hypertension is:

 a. Egg soup diet . . . . □

 b. Grapefruit diet . . . . □

 c. DASH diet . . . . □

 d. HCG diet . . . . □

33. Which is a possible side effect of zinc supplements?

 a. Increased HDL . . . . □

    b.   Decreased triglycerides . . . . ☐

    c.   Decreased HDL. . . . . ☐

    d.   Increased triglycerides . . . . ☐

34. What fluid is best if you exercise for less than sixty minutes?

    a.   Sports drink (6% glucose solution) . . . . ☐

    b.   Water . . . . ☐

    c.   Both A and B are equally effective. . . . . ☐

    d.   None is correct . . . . ☐

35. In nutrition, the acronym "UL" stands for:

    a.   Recommended dietary allowance . . . . ☐

    b.   Upper tolerable limit . . . . ☐

    c.   Minimum intake . . . . ☐

    d.   Unusually low in a nutrient . . . . ☐

36. Possible side effects of high protein diets in healthy people include:

    a.   Osteoporosis . . . . ☐

    b.   Liver damage . . . . ☐

    c.   Dehydration . . . . ☐

    d.   None are correct. . . . . ☐

37. Which food provides the most complex carbohydrates?

    a.   Steak, 8 oz. . . . . ☐

    b.   Chicken, 8 oz . . . . ☐

    c.   Salmon, 8 oz . . . . ☐

    d.   None . . . . ☐

38. Possible side effects from low carb diets can include:

    a.   Ketosis . . . . ☐

    b.   Dehydration . . . . ☐

    c.   Glycogen loss . . . . ☐

    d.   All are correct . . . . ☐

39. A method used to increase glycogen synthesis is:

    a.   Carbohydrate loading . . . . ☐

    b.   Glycogen super-compensation . . . . ☐

    c.   Glutamine-enhanced oxidative respiration . . . . ☐

    d.   Both A and B are correct . . . . ☐

40. A rating scale that shows how fast carbohydrates are absorbed is called the:

    a.   Glucose absorption scale . . . . ☐

    b.   Simple sugar index . . . . ☐

    c.   Glycemic index . . . . ☐

    d.   Both B and C are correct . . . . ☐

41. Which is true concerning vitamins?

    a.   People who work out intensely need more vitamins . . . . . ☐

    b.   Even in those who eat a healthy diet, vitamins speed up recovery after exercise . . . ☐

    c.   Vitamin needs for men and women are significantly different . . . . ☐

    d.   None are true . . . . ☐

42. Your client tells you he smells like ammonia after his workout. You suspect he is:

    a.   Eating a low carb diet . . . . ☐

    b.   Not eating enough protein . . . . ☐

    c.   Lacking branch chain amino acids . . . . ☐

    d.   Deficient in glutamine . . . . ☐

43. A hormone which increases RBC production is:

    a.   Erythropoietin (EPO) . . . . ☐

    b.   Atrial natriuretic peptide (ANF) . . . . ☐

    c.   Glycogen synthase . . . . ☐

    d.   Phosphofructokinase (PFK) . . . . ☐

44. Which B vitamin can help reduce birth defects?

    a.   Folate . . . . ☐

    b.   Folic acid . . . . ☐

    c.   Iron . . . . ☐

    d.   Both A and B are correct . . . . ☐

45. Which of the following is not a result of drinking water?

    a.   Muscle contraction . . . . ☐

    b.   Lubrication of joints . . . . ☐

    c.   Decrease in fatigue . . . . ☐

    d.   All are correct . . . . ☐

46. After a marathon, your client has lost five pounds. Which is an appropriate fluid replacement guideline?

    a.   8 oz per pound lost . . . . ☐

    b.   16 oz per pound lost . . . . ☐

    c.   24 oz per pound lost . . . . ☐

    d.   32 oz per pound lost . . . . ☐

47. Which ingredient in energy drinks is mostly responsible for increased alertness?

    a.   Taurine . . . . ☐

    b.   Tyrosine . . . . ☐

    c.   Caffeine . . . . ☐

    d.   Branch chain amino acids . . . . ☐

48. Which is a sign of hyponatremia?

    a.   Confusion . . . . ☐

    b.   Headaches . . . . ☐

    c.   Nausea and vomiting . . . . ☐

    d.   All are correct . . . . ☐

49. Your client asks for diet advice. Which would be the overall best answer?

    a.   Eat more protein . . . . ☐

    b.   Reduce carbs from the diet . . . . ☐

    c.   Reduce calories by a little less than usually eaten . . . . ☐

    d.   Exercise every day for forty-five minutes . . . . ☐

50. If weight loss is the goal, what is a healthy amount to lose per week?

    a.   1–2 lbs. per week . . . . ☐

    b.   3–4 lbs. per week . . . . ☐

    c.   4–5 lbs. per week . . . . ☐

    d.   5–6 lbs. per week . . . . ☐

51. Which of the following is not considered part of female athletic triad?

    a.   Osteoporosis . . . . ☐

    b.   Eating disorders . . . . ☐

    c.   Menstrual disturbances . . . . ☐

    d.   Diabetes . . . . ☐

52. Which supplement is also considered a pro-hormone?

    a.   Glutamine . . . . ☐

    b.   Vitamin D . . . . ☐

    c.   Vitamin K. . . . . □

    d.   Tryptophan . . . . □

53. Which is considered an acceptable/healthy level of cholesterol?

    a.   240 mg/dl. . . . . □

    b.   220 mg/dl. . . . . □

    c.   200 mg/dl. . . . . □

    d.   190 mg/dl. . . . . □

54. Which can raise triglyceride levels?

    a.   Cigarette smoking. . . . . □

    b.   High carb diets . . . . □

    c.   Type II diabetes . . . . □

    d.   All of the above . . . . □

55. People with hypertension should reduce sodium intake to less than:

    a.   5200 mg per day . . . . □

    b.   4500 mg per day . . . . □

    c.   2300 mg per day . . . . □

    d.   1050 mg per day . . . . □

56. Which vitamin can give urine a yellow appearance?

    a.   Vitamin C. . . . . □

    b.   Folic acid . . . . □

    c.   Riboflavin . . . . □

    d.   Niacin. . . . . □

57. Which can play a role in how much protein someone might need?

    a.   Body weight. . . . . □

    b.   Age . . . . □

    c.   Training status . . . . □

    d.   All are correct . . . . □

58. What do most diets all have in common?

    a.   They reduce carbs . . . . □

    b.   They reduce calories . . . . □

    c.   They reduce fat . . . . □

    d.   None are correct. . . . . □

59. **In a healthy diet, protein should make up which percentage of calories per day:**

    a.   10%–12% . . . . ☐

    b.   12%–15% . . . . ☐

    c.   15%–20% . . . . ☐

    d.   20%–30% . . . . ☐

60. **Which is often considered a conditionally essential amino acid?**

    a.   Leucine . . . . ☐

    b.   Glutamine. . . . . ☐

    c.   Tryptophan . . . . ☐

    d.   Isoleucine . . . . ☐

You've reached the end of this section—and the end of the test!

Answers to the Test

Answers: Exercise Science Section

1. Krebs cycle
2. Fasciculus
3. Sarcomere
4. Sarcoplasmic reticulum
5. Anaerobic
6. Troponin
7. None are correct
8. ATPase
9. Type IIb
10. Actin
11. Type II fibers
12. NEAT
13. Mitochondria
14. Type IIb fibers
15. Slow twitch/Type I fibers
16. Valsalva maneuver
17. Sliding filament theory
18. Sarcopenia
19. Breathing
20. Increase in muscle size
21. Hyperplasia
22. Lower RHR
23. Increased RBCs
24. Muscle soreness
25. Rhabdomyolysis (See http://www.joe-cannon.com/rhabdomylysis)
26. Increase in breathing rate after exercise
27. Anabolism + catabolism
28. Cardiac output
29. Increased BP
30. Atrophy
31. Push-ups
32. Metabolic equivalents

33. Erythrocytes and RBCs are the same thing
34. Lower BP
35. Type IIa
36. Variable resistance
37. Humerus is a bone, not a muscle
38. All are false
39. Maximum lifts that also stress low back
40. Both B and C are correct
41. Excitation/contraction coupling
42. Acetylcholine
43. Aorta
44. Motor nerve and all the fibers it stimulates
45. Type I fibers
46. Cortisol
47. Thyroid gland
48. Pancreas
49. Pituitary gland
50. ADP
51. True
52. IGF (insulin-like growth factors)
53. All are correct
54. Capillaries
55. Cardiac output = Heart rate x Stroke volume
56. Lactate
57. Tendon placement and muscle fiber type
58. ATP/CP and phosphagen system are the same
59. All are correct
60. Pericardium

Answers: Anatomy and Physiology Section

1. Left ventricle
2. Golgi tendon organ (GTO)
3. Ligament
4. Right atrium
5. SA node
6. Both A and B are correct
7. Right ventricle
8. Osteoarthritis
9. All are correct
10. Arteries (think "A" for "away")
11. Hemoglobin
12. Osteoclast
13. Both B and C are correct
14. 206 bones
15. Brain
16. Bone marrow
17. Both A and B are correct
18. Treadmill
19. Buttocks
20. Type I fibers
21. Glycogen
22. Both A and C are correct
23. All are correct
24. None are correct
25. Humerus
26. All are correct
27. Supination
28. Lack of exercise/too many calories consumed
29. Heart disease
30. Both B and C are correct
31. Sympathetic NS
32. Shoulder

33. Walking
34. Helps increase bone strength
35. Articular cartilage
36. 80% 10RM
37. Lower RHR
38. C is correct
39. C is correct
40. Eccentric
41. Vasodilation
42. 7.4 pH
43. Metabolic syndrome
44. Chemoreceptors
45. Cardiac output
46. 100,000 miles of blood vessels
47. Transverse plane
48. Abduction
49. False
50. Type IIa fibers
51. Sympathetic nervous system
52. Type 1 fibers are oxidative
53. Joint
54. Isokinetic
55. Ejection fraction
56. Both A and B are correct
57. End diastolic volume
58. Tendons connect muscles to bones
59. Muscles can only pull
60. Myofibrils

Answers: Fitness Testing Section

1. All are correct
2. 35 ml O2/kg BW/min
3. Men < 40 inches; women < 35 inches
4. 1 RM
5. None are correct
6. 10 minutes elliptical
7. Decrease muscle power
8. 1.5 mile run
9. 18.5–24.9
10. All are correct
11. Above 45 mg/dl
12. Body fat
13. Prehypertension
14. Tachycardia
15. 60–100 bpm
16. Thumb side of wrist (radial pulse)
17. Hydrostatic weighing
18. None are correct
19. Both A and B are correct
20. Both A and B are correct
21. Repetition maximum
22. Muscular endurance
23. Metabolic rate 5x higher than resting
24. 140/90 mm Hg
25. Sit quietly for 5–10 minutes
26. Blood pressure meds
27. Osteoporosis
28. Obesity
29. Top number
30. Aerobic fitness
31. Body mass index
32. All are correct

33. PAR Q
34. High BMI
35. Take from right side of body
36. Myocardial infarction (MI)
37. Heart disease (Coronary Artery Disease)
38. Obtain medical clearance before training client
39. Hypertension (high blood pressure)
40. Estimates exercise heart rate
41. Avoid because of side effects
42. Both A and B are correct
43. Stop the test is safest option
44. More DOMS (muscle soreness)
45. Waivers are likely not valid when signed by minors
46. Ligamentous laxity
47. All are correct
48. Localized muscle endurance
49. Agility
50. Atherosclerosis (hardening of the arteries)
51. All over the above are correct
52. Insulin resistance, AKA metabolic syndrome/type II diabetes
53. After they exhale normally
54. All of the above can be a source of error
55. Both B and C are correct
56. All of the above
57. Cardiovascular (aerobic) endurance
58. Grip strength
59. The greater the fitness level
60. 11 METs ($39 \div 3.5 = 11$)

Answers: Exercise Program Design Section

1. Periodization
2. Muscle endurance
3. Treadmill 4days/week
4. None are correct
5. Endurance, hypertrophy, strength, power
6. Both A and B
7. Lat pulldown/bench press
8. Bench, lat pulldown, leg press, hamstring curl
9. 6–7 days per week
10. 2–3 days per week
11. 2–3 weeks
12. Termination of exercise
13. Both A and B are correct
14. 80% VO2 max
15. Running
16. <30s
17. Muscle hypertrophy
18. reps x sets x weight
19. False
20. RPE
21. Circuit training
22. 220 – age – RHR x percent of desired heart rate + RHR
23. 170
24. Both A and C are correct
25. 138 to 164 bpm
26. Soleus
27. Leg press
28. Leg press
29. Leg press
30. Brachialis
31. Flexibility
32. Warm up, then stretch

33. Bench press at a reduced weight (e.g. 40% 10RM)
34. Alternated grip
35. All are errors
36. Rhomboids and posterior deltoids
37. Body composition
38. Drop in blood pressure upon rising
39. Less DOMS
40. None are correct
41. Both A and C are correct
42. Leg press, chest press, lat pulldown, shoulder press
43. Get doctor's permission before training begins
44. Call 911 and perform CPR/AED
45. All are correct
46. Bones; BMD = bone mineral density
47. All are correct
48. 60%–80% of 1 RM
49. Increase the reps performed before increasing the weight lifted
50. Circuit training
51. Rheumatoid arthritis
52. All are principles of exercise
53. Familiarity with RPE increases its accuracy
54. OBLA = onset of blood lactate accumulation
55. Aim for 60 minutes of activity on the treadmill if possible
56. Plyometrics
57. Leg curl machine
58. This BP is very high. See doctor before returning to exercise.
59. None of those tests are appropriate
60. Leg press

Answers: Nutrition and Sports Nutrition

1. 4, 4, 9
2. Hyponatremia
3. 28
4. Zero
5. 0.4 g/lb
6. None are correct (See http://supplement-geek.com/creatine-injuries)
7. Carbs
8. 20 miles
9. None are correct (See http://www.joe-cannon.com/supplement)
10. Creatine monohydrate
11. Less than 30%
12. 0.6 g/lb.–0.9 g/lb.
13. Recommended dietary allowance
14. Vitamins A, E, D, and K
15. Non essential amino acid (See http://supplement-geek.com/glutamine-review)
16. Leucine, isoleucine, and valine
17. False
18. 3500
19. None: They are all equal
20. Water loss (See http://www.joe-cannon.com/low-carb)
21. 0.6 grams per pound
22. Supplements do have regulations that apply
23. Glutamine
24. Type IIb fibers
25. Improve exercise performance
26. Marathon runner
27. All are correct
28. Beta carotene
29. 20–30 grams per day
30. The human body does not make vitamins
31. Resting metabolic rate (RMR)
32. DASH diet

33. Decreased HDL levels
34. Water
35. Upper tolerable limit
36. Dehydration
37. None are sources of complex carbs
38. All are correct
39. Carbohydrate loading and glycogen super-compensation
40. Glycemic index
41. None are true
42. They may be eating a low carb diet
43. Erythropoietin (EPO)
44. Both folic acid and folate
45. Water helps all of these conditions
46. Consume 24 oz. per pound that is lost
47. Caffeine
48. All are signs of hyponatremia
49. Reduce calories
50. Not more than 1–2 pounds per week
51. Diabetes
52. Vitamin D
53. Less than 200 mg/dl is desirable so 190 is the answer
54. All can raise triglyceride levels
55. Less 2300 mg per day (For some, it's less than 1500 mg per day)
56. Riboflavin
57. All can play a role in protein requirements
58. Most diets are low in calories
59. 12% to 15% for most healthy people
60. Glutamine may be conditionally essential in some situations

Scoring
Section

Count the number of correct answers from each section and write them in the appropriate "*Your Score*" space provided. For example, if you had 48 correct answers in the Exercise Science section, write 48 under the "88–80" column. A score of 48 would equal 80% correct for that section (48/60 = 80%). Do this for each section of the test.

Scoring: Exercise Science Section

% correct	100–90	88–80	78–70	68–60	58–50	≤48%
# correct	60–54	53–48	47–42	41–36	35–30	≤29
Your score						

80% or better = passing

Scoring: Anatomy and Physiology Section

% correct	100–90	88–80	78–70	68–60	58–50	≤48%
# correct	60–54	53–48	47–42	41–36	35–30	≤29
Your score						

80% or better = passing

Scoring: Fitness Testing Section

% correct	100–90	88–80	78–70	68–60	58–50	≤49%
# correct	60–54	53–48	47–42	41–36	35–30	≤29
Your score						

80% or better = passing

Scoring: Exercise Program Design Section

% correct	100–90	88–80	78–70	68–60	58–50	≤49%
# correct	60–54	53–48	47–42	41–36	35–30	≤29
Your score						

80% or better = passing

Scoring: Nutrition/Sports Nutrition Section

% correct	100–90	88–80	78–70	68–60	58–50	≤49%
# correct	60–54	53–48	47–42	41–36	35–30	≤29
Your score						

80% or better = passing

Overall Scoring: How Did You Do In Each Section?

How did you do in each section? To find out, copy your number of correct answers from each section into the "# of correct answers" column. Compare this to the "# needed to pass" column. This will give you a quick overview of your strengths and weaknesses.

Section	Your # of correct answers	Minimum # needed to pass
Exercise Science		48
Anatomy & Physiology		48
Fitness Testing		48
Exercise Program Design		48
Nutrition & Sports Nutrition		48

How Did You Do?

A score of 48 = 80% correct in a section. 54 correct answers = 90% correct. A score of 57 = 95% and, of course, 60 out of 60 correct is a perfect score of 100%.

Remember, many certification exams require a score of at least 80% to pass. So, if you scored 80% on this practice test, I recommend you keep studying because you are on the fence.
Remember also, if you fail the real test, you may have to pay either the entire amount again or a part of the amount when you retest. The organization through which you take the examination can give you more information on this.

Top 25 Tips

How to Take a Certification Exam

1. Go to the Facebook page of the organization and ask questions about the test.

2. Check Amazon to see if you can get the study materials for a cheaper price.

3. Try to find the name of the teacher of the certification course. They may have a website where you can find tips on the testing process.

4. Use Google maps to see what the location of the testing facility looks like. This will save you time finding the location.

5. Highlight the textbook and take notes.

6. Summarize each chapter in the textbook with the most important information.

7. Improve retention of material by asking yourself, "Would any of my clients ever ask me this?" This prepares you to better absorb the material because you've put yourself in a real-life situation.

8. The night before the test, get sufficient sleep.

9. If you are traveling to an unfamiliar area to take the exam, give yourself extra time to get to the location.

10. Remember to bring your ID and CPR/AED cards to the certification. Some organizations won't let you take the exam unless you have these.

11. Bring ear plugs. This simple tip will help you concentrate better if you are taking a test in a room full of people.

12. Bring a calculator. Some fitness organizations require you to do mathematical calculations during the test. Ask the organization if a calculator will be needed.

13. Turn off your cell phone and keep it out of sight. All organizations take cheating very seriously.

14. Make flash cards out of the notes you take to help you study more effectively.

15. Don't listen to others who say, "You don't need to know that for the test." Fitness organizations usually have different versions of the exam.

16. If the fitness organization has practice tests of their own available for purchase, I recommend you get them. The questions they ask may be more representative of the actual questions you will see. This test has a Resource Page that lists several practice tests. Here is the link: http://www.joe-cannon.com/test-resources

17. Don't be afraid to call the organization and ask them questions if something doesn't make sense in what you are studying. Also, post questions you have on their Facebook page.

18. Check out ITunes University. It's part of ITunes. There is a free college course on exercise science. Its 100% free!

19. Don't prepare by reading bodybuilding magazines or websites. Personal training is not the same as bodybuilding. You need to have a personal training text book.

20. Don't assume that because you like to work out you will pass without studying. All certifications are heavily grounded in science which you need to know in order to pass.

21. Before deciding what certificate is right for you, go to local gyms and ask what certifications they accept. Not all gyms accept all certs.

22. Don't pay a gym for their certification because it's likely that nobody else will accept it.

23. Be careful with online fitness certifications. Many gyms will not accept online certifications that you receive by taking exams from the privacy of your own home.

24. Time yourself. Most certification exams have a time limit.

25. Remember, many certs usually expire every one or two years. Get re-certified **before** it expires. Find out what it takes to get recertified.

Bonus Tip

26. Remember, getting certified is the easy part. Being *certified* and *qualified* are not the same. Continuing to educate yourself *after* you get certified is the best way to become a successful personal trainer.

My Books

I've written several books—including a personal training book—that can help you. You can see them all here: http://www.joe-cannon.com/books

What Did You Think?

Did this test help? I hope so. If you have any questions you can contact me from my website: http://www.joe-cannon.com/contact/

Made in the USA
Columbia, SC
05 August 2018